VOLCANOES

Written by Emily Dodd

Contents

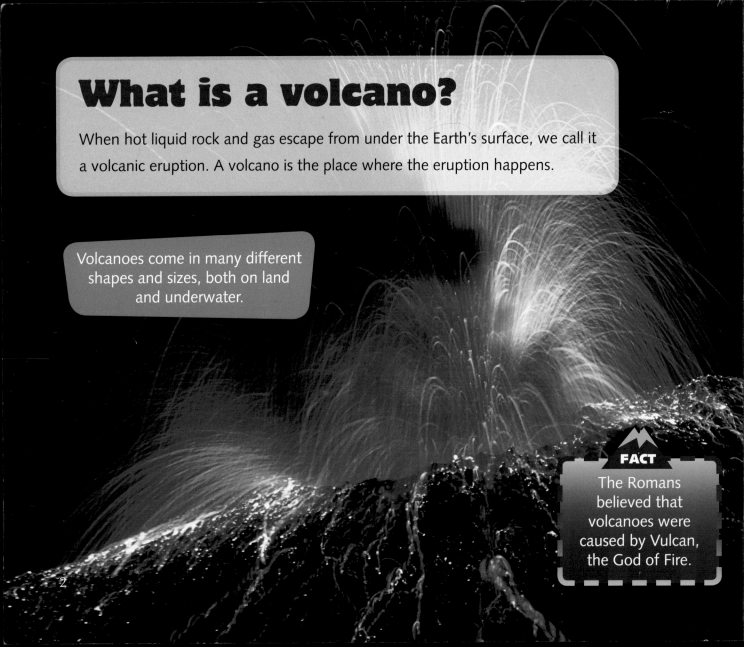

What is a volcano?

When hot liquid rock and gas escape from under the Earth's surface, we call it a volcanic eruption. A volcano is the place where the eruption happens.

Volcanoes come in many different shapes and sizes, both on land and underwater.

FACT

The Romans believed that volcanoes were caused by Vulcan, the God of Fire.

When rock gets so hot that it melts and becomes liquid we call it molten rock. The molten rock found in volcanoes is known as magma when it's inside the volcano underground, and lava when it erupts out of the volcano above ground.

When molten rock eventually cools, it becomes solid rock.

3

Volcanic eruptions

There are two main types of volcanic eruption – effusive and explosive.

Effusive eruptions are slow and gentle with runny lava that flows away from the volcano.

Explosive volcanoes are much more violent. Gases build up in the thick, slowly flowing magma underground until eventually they explode out of the volcano. These explosions force volcanic **ash**, gas and lumps of lava into the surrounding area.

With every eruption, volcanoes change shape. There are volcanic eruptions happening right now, somewhere on Earth.

Active volcanoes erupt regularly.

Volcano states

When an active volcano isn't erupting we say it is **dormant**.
Volcanoes stop erupting when the magma beneath
them stops moving. When a volcano
last erupted more than 10,000 years
ago, we say it's extinct and it's not
expected to erupt ever again.

Edinburgh Castle is built on
the remains of an extinct volcano.

Inside the Earth

To find out what causes volcanic eruptions, we need to look inside the Earth.

Planet Earth was once molten, but the outer layer has now cooled to form solid rock. The outer layer is called the crust.

FACT

If the Earth were the size of an apple, the crust would be about the thickness of the apple's skin.

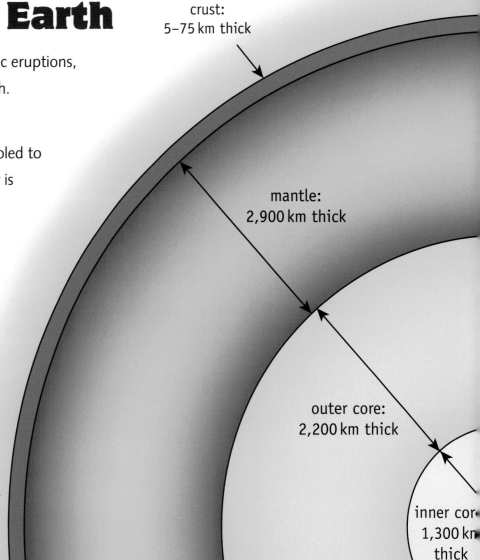

crust:
5–75 km thick

mantle:
2,900 km thick

outer core:
2,200 km thick

inner cor
1,300 km
thick

At the very centre of our planet is a ball made of two types of metal – iron and nickel. It's called the core.

Surrounding the core is the mantle. It's made of hot rock. That rock becomes lighter as it heats up and it moves slowly up towards the surface of the Earth where it cools and sinks towards the core again.

FACT

The Earth's core is hotter than the surface of the Sun!

The Earth's crust

On land, the Earth's crust is 10 to 75 kilometres thick and it's covered with soil, plants and buildings. The crust is much thinner in the oceans – around seven kilometres thick and covered in sea water.

The crust is split into huge sections called plates. As the hot rock in the mantle moves, the plates move too. We find most volcanoes around the edges of plates.

Explosive eruptions happen where plates are moving towards each other. Effusive eruptions happen where plates are moving away from each other. Sometimes effusive eruptions happen in the middle of plates too – these are called hot spot volcanoes.

FACT
The Earth's plates move around 2.5 centimetres per year, which is the speed your fingernails grow.

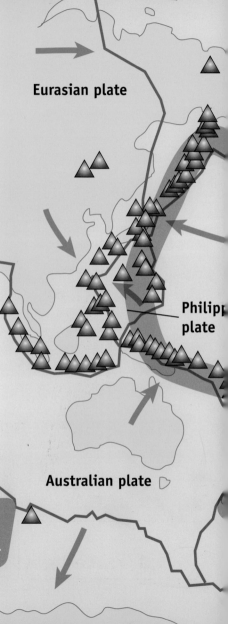

Eurasian plate

Philippine plate

Australian plate

The map shows the plates that make up the Earth's crust, and the direction they're moving.

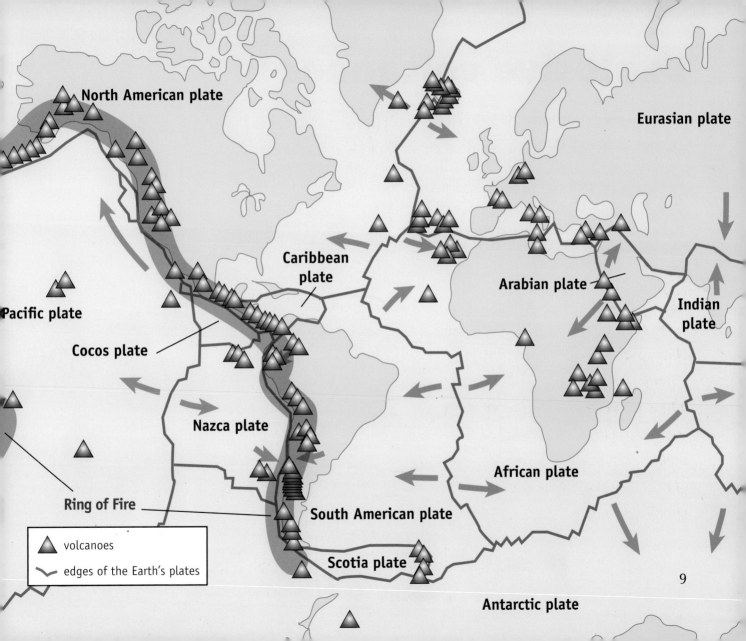

North American plate

Eurasian plate

Pacific plate

Cocos plate

Caribbean plate

Arabian plate

Indian plate

Nazca plate

African plate

Ring of Fire

South American plate

Scotia plate

Antarctic plate

△ volcanoes

⌄ edges of the Earth's plates

9

Explosive volcanoes

As the plates collide, the thinner underwater plate is pulled under the thicker plate on land. Heat and sea water cause the mantle around the thinner plate to melt.

As the plates continue to push against each other, the force causes crumpling and folding in the thicker plate. Over millions of years, this creates mountain ranges.

Volcanoes form inside these mountains as the gassy magma pushes its way up to the surface through cracks in the rock. The thick, sticky magma cools, plugging the gap at the top until eventually the pressure is so great that there is an explosion of rock, gas and ash.

Explosive eruptions can be one huge explosion or lots of smaller explosions.

There is a circle of explosive volcanoes around the Pacific Ocean called the Ring of Fire.

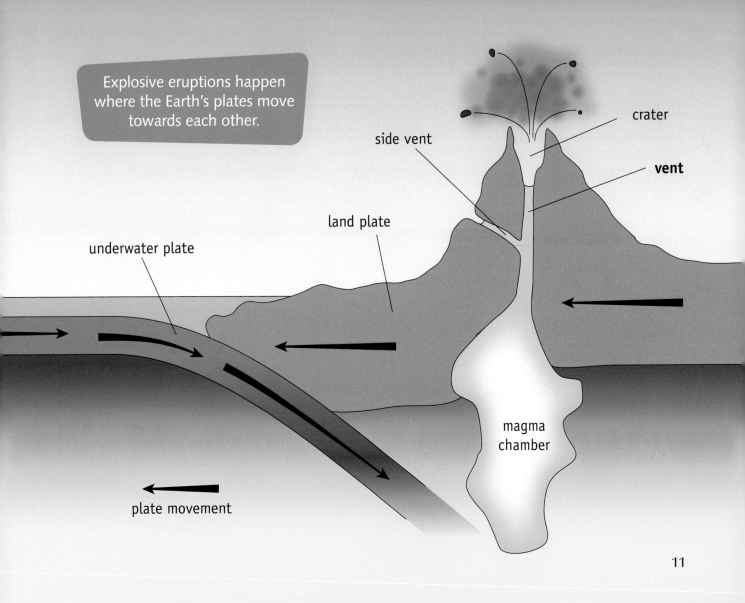

Explosive eruptions happen where the Earth's plates move towards each other.

crater

side vent

vent

land plate

underwater plate

plate movement

magma chamber

11

Stratovolcanoes

Explosive volcanoes can erupt following a pattern, with an ash eruption followed by a lava eruption and then another ash eruption. When this continues, ash and lava are set down in layers around the volcano and we call it a stratovolcano.

FACT

"Strata" is the Latin word for layers. More than half the world's volcanoes are stratovolcanoes.

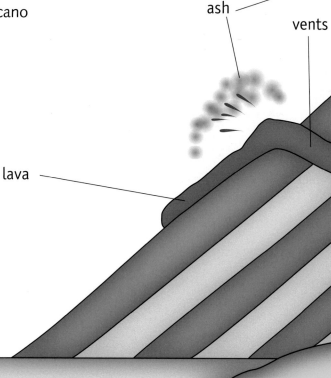

ash

vents

lava

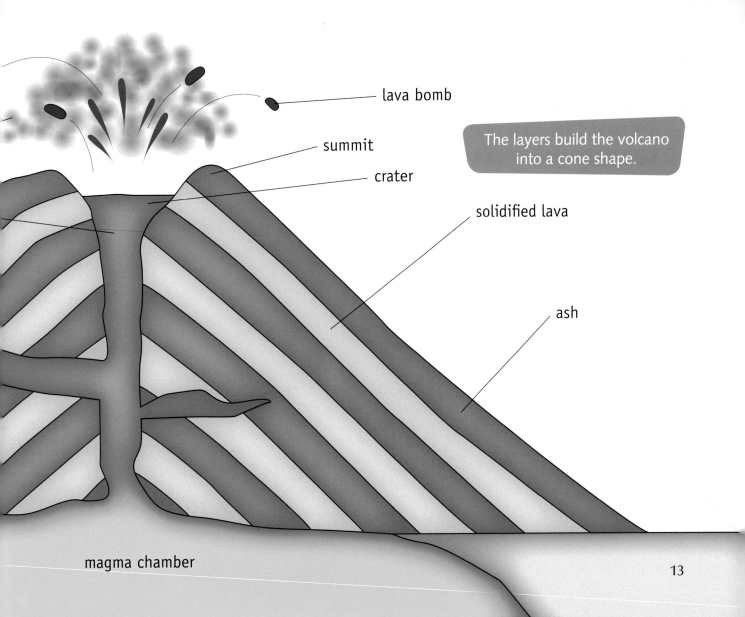

lava bomb

summit

crater

The layers build the volcano
into a cone shape.

solidified lava

ash

magma chamber

13

Mount St Helens
Washington State, USA

Mount St Helens is an example of an explosive stratovolcano. It erupted on 18th May 1980, after lying dormant for 123 years.

An earthquake caused a landslide, and the top 400 metres of the mountain exploded sideways into thick black clouds of ash, gas and rock that destroyed everything in their path.

Snow and ice mixed with the ash, causing mudslides.

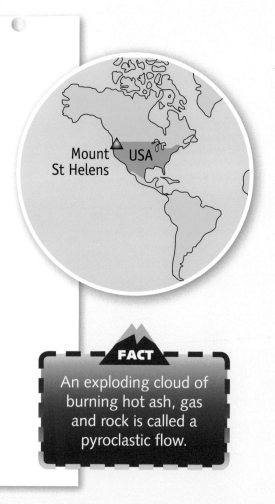

FACT

An exploding cloud of burning hot ash, gas and rock is called a pyroclastic flow.

Mount St Helens eruption, 1980

In the two months leading up to the eruption, scientists observed 1,500 small earthquakes. That meant the magma was moving inside the mountain. There were also some small steam eruptions, and the scientists noticed the mountain was growing in height. Scientists expected an eruption was on the way. Using evidence from previous eruptions, they predicted a safe zone 7 kilometres around the volcano centre.

When the volcano erupted, the blast spread further than the scientists expected and 57 people were killed.

The blast was so strong that it uprooted every tree within 8 kilometres of the volcano.

Effusive volcanoes

In effusive eruptions, the lava is thin and fast flowing. It can travel for several kilometres on land before it cools to form solid rock. If there's another eruption, the next layer of lava cools and solidifies on top of the earlier one. Gradually volcanoes grow into the shape of an upturned shield.

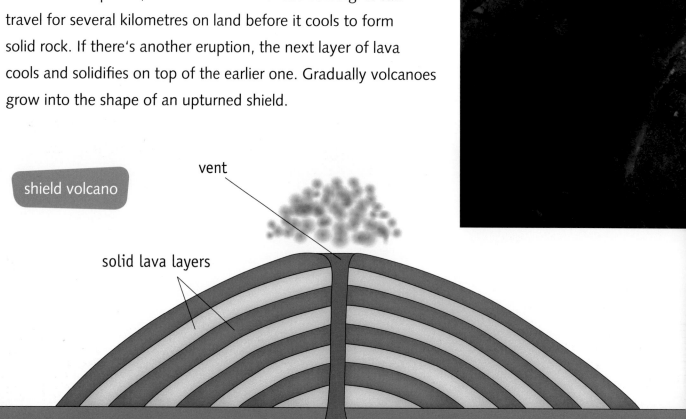

shield volcano

vent

solid lava layers

crust

magma chamber

Hot molten pillow lava erupting from an underwater lava tube at the ocean entry of Kilauea Volcano on Hawaii Island, Hawaii

Effusive eruptions can happen on land and underwater. There's a row of effusive volcanoes along the middle of the Atlantic Ocean called the Mid-Atlantic Ridge. These volcanoes are continually erupting. When effusive volcanoes erupt underwater, the sea water quickly cools the lava. Unusual rock formations occur, like pillow lava.

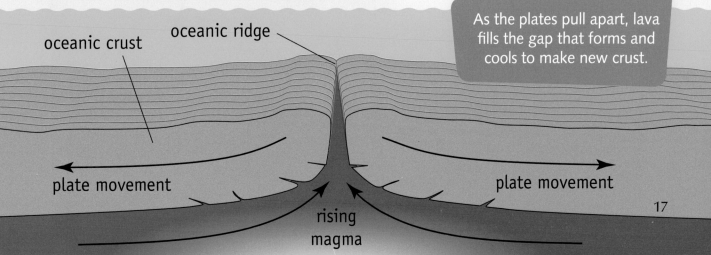

oceanic crust

oceanic ridge

As the plates pull apart, lava fills the gap that forms and cools to make new crust.

plate movement

plate movement

rising magma

Iceland

Iceland was created by
effusive volcanoes erupting
along the Mid-Atlantic
Ridge. It is the most volcanically
active island on Earth. Iceland is one
of the few places you can see new crust
being created on land, so it's a good place
to go and study volcanoes.

Iceland

North
American
Plate

Eurasian
Plate

ICELAND

Reykjavik

Mid-Atlantic
Ridge

Atlantic
Ocean

Effusive volcanoes
continually erupt
through vents and
along long cracks in the
ground called fissures.

18

Iceland is still growing as the plates pull away from each other, forming new land in the gap as the lava cools.

Icelanders are warned to stay indoors if dangerous gases are being blown towards them. If large quantities of ash erupt into the sky, aeroplanes are rerouted away from the area.

Most of the time, people in Iceland live comfortably with volcanoes. They're even useful! The volcanoes heat up water in the ground and create hot springs, which can be used for bathing, central heating and generating electricity.

Much of Iceland is made up of huge lava fields.

Hot spot volcanoes

Hot spot volcanoes erupt in the middle of Earth's plates –
on land and underwater. They are usually effusive eruptions.

Hot spot volcanoes are
created when an area of hot
magma builds up beneath
the crust. The magma
eventually punches through
the crust.

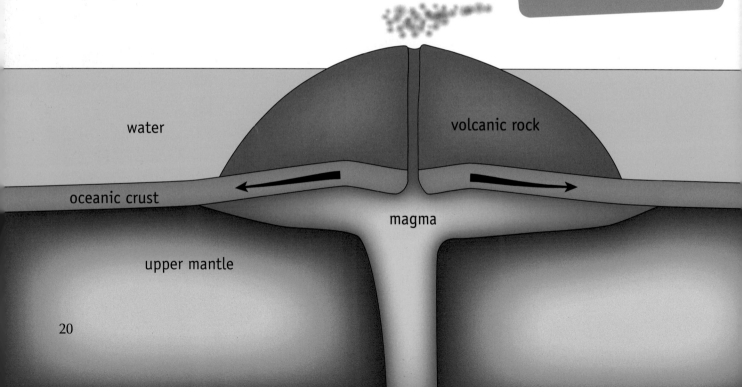

water

volcanic rock

oceanic crust

magma

upper mantle

If hot spot volcanoes continue to erupt underwater, they can create new islands. This is how Hawaii was created.

FACT

Volcanic islands have black sand made from **eroded** volcanic rock.

Hawaii
Pacific Ocean

The islands of Hawaii are the tips of volcanoes created by a hot spot.

Over time, the Earth's crust slowly moves over the hot spot and the magma punches new holes, creating the Hawaiian chain of islands.

Hawaii

The newest islands form when the hot spot volcano erupts directly beneath them.

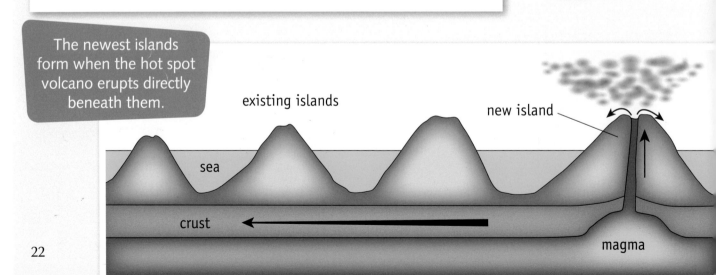

existing islands

new island

sea

crust

magma

We normally measure mountain height starting at sea level but if instead we measure from base to tip, Mauna Kea in Hawaii is the tallest mountain on Earth – standing at 10,210 metres tall. That's even taller than Mount Everest!

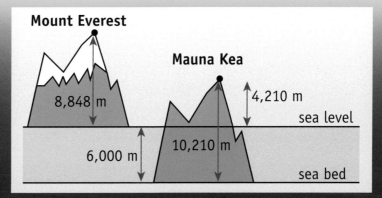

Mount Everest

Mauna Kea

8,848 m

4,210 m

sea level

6,000 m

10,210 m

sea bed

Mount Everest

Mauna Kea

Volcano geology

granite

By studying the chemistry and crystals in volcanic rocks, we can work out what type of volcano they came from.

Granite is formed by explosive volcanoes. Magma cools slowly underground giving the crystals time to grow large. Many buildings are made from granite.

the city of Aberdeen in Scotland, known as the Granite City

Basalt is formed by effusive volcanoes. The lava cools more quickly, forming smaller crystals. Earth's underwater crust is made from basalt.

basalt

Sometimes lava cools very quickly to form obsidian, a black volcanic glass. Stone Age people used obsidian to make spearheads. Today, surgeons use it on the tips of their **scalpels**.

obsidian spearhead

The gassy lava in explosive volcanoes creates a pale coloured rock called pumice. The bubbles make pumice so light that it floats. You may find it washed up on a beach, a long way from a volcano.

Sometimes blobs of lava are flung high into the air during a violent volcanic eruption. These blobs are called lava bombs.

Lava bombs can be as big as a car.

FACT

People use pumice to rub dry skin off their feet.

Predicting eruptions

Scientists who study volcanoes are called volcanologists.

Volcanologists measure the size and shape of previous lava flows to work out how much lava was released, which direction the lava flowed and if the volcano was explosive or effusive.

When lava explodes, it forms volcanic ash.

Volcanologists also investigate temperature, chemistry and movements in volcanoes.

Following the eruption of Mount St Helens, the ash spread across eleven states.

26

By studying soil samples, volcanologists work out how much ash was released and how far it travelled. This information helps them predict safe zones around erupting volcanoes.

Scientists monitor volcanoes for earthquakes. Earthquakes are a sign that magma is moving; they often occur around a volcano before an eruption.

By analysing the mud deposits from previous eruptions, scientists work out how far the lahar flowed and how much ash the volcano produced.

Volcanic ash mixes with water to create mud flows called lahars.

Montserrat
Caribbean Sea

Montserrat

Scientists were monitoring Chances Peak volcano on the island of Montserrat. When it erupted in 1995, they were prepared.

Before the main eruption, there were many small earthquakes and eruptions of dust and ash.

Scientists believed that the island's population were in danger, so around 11,000 people were evacuated before the eruption.

A few people refused to leave and 19 of them died as a result.

Chances Peak remained active for five years, making it impossible for residents to return.

Pyroclastic flows covered the town in ash and mud. Many buildings, including the hospital and airport, were destroyed.

The volcano stopped erupting in 2000 and scientists decided it was safe for islanders to return. Since then, new roads, a new airport and a volcanic observatory have been built and the volcano has become a tourist attraction.

Volcanoes and earthquakes

An increase in the frequency of earthquakes warned scientists that Mount St Helens and Chances Peak might erupt. Magma inside the volcanoes was pushing its way up towards the surface, causing the surrounding rock to crack and shake.

Earthquakes often happen around the edges of the Earth's plates.

North American plate

Eurasian plate

● earthquakes

⌄ edges of the Earth's plates

Caribbean plate

Philippine plate

Pacific plate

Arabian plate

Cocos plate

Pacific plat

Indian plate

Nazca plate

African plate

Australian plate

South American plate

Antarctic plate

30

Scotia plate

Magma moving in volcanoes isn't the only way earthquakes are made. As plates move past each other, they sometimes get stuck and suddenly jolt. We feel this jolt as an earthquake.

Earthquakes can be dangerous but they also help scientists to understand a little bit more about the inside of our planet.

When an earthquake occurs, the shaking vibrations travel through the inside of the Earth and along its surface. Earthquake vibrations travel at different speeds through different materials.

By measuring the speed at which earthquake vibrations travel, scientists can investigate and predict the hidden structure inside the Earth.

damage caused by the earthquake in Christchurch, New Zealand, 2011

Volcanic disasters
Mount Vesuvius, Italy

In the year 79 CE one of the most famous volcanoes of all time erupted in southern Italy.

Mount Vesuvius erupted and buried the nearby towns of Pompeii and Herculaneum in more than two metres of ash. Pompeii and Herculaneum remained buried, frozen in time until the 18th century when **archaeologists** and scientists began to **excavate** the city. They discovered thousands of people had been killed almost instantly by pyroclastic flows from Mount Vesuvius.

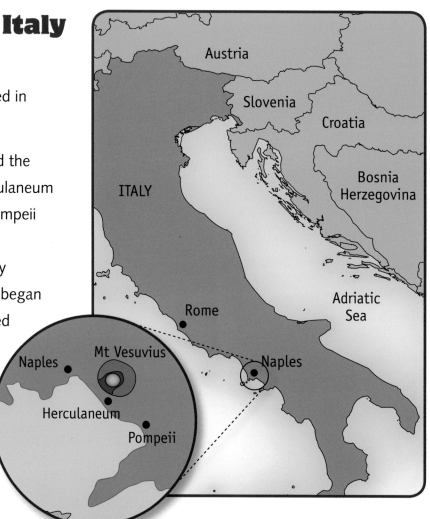

Austria

Slovenia

Croatia

Bosnia Herzegovina

ITALY

Adriatic Sea

Rome

Naples

Mt Vesuvius

Naples

Herculaneum

Pompeii

Over the centuries, the bodies decayed leaving a hollow space inside the rock. Archaeologists poured plaster of Paris into the holes to make casts of the people in the position they were in when they died.

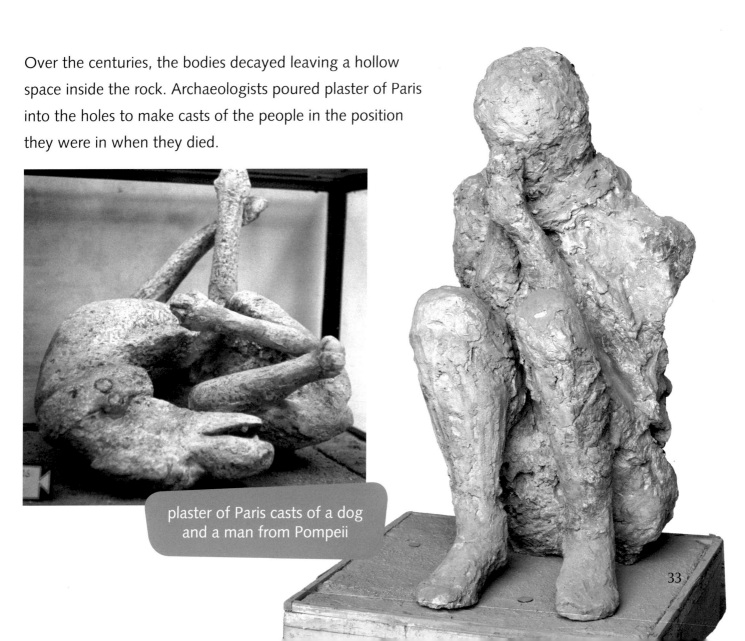

plaster of Paris casts of a dog and a man from Pompeii

Krakatoa, Indonesia

In 1883, three volcanic peaks on the island of Krakatoa in Indonesia exploded in the most violent volcanic eruption in known history.

The island exploded into the sea causing tsunamis (huge waves) to travel through the water.

Indonesia

Krakatoa

The eruption destroyed two thirds of Krakatoa and the dust from the volcano rose high into Earth's **atmosphere**, blocking out the sun's light and changing weather patterns all around the world.

The tsunamis killed more than 36,000 people in the surrounding area.

Nevado del Ruiz, South America

In 1985, Nevado del Ruiz erupted in Colombia in South America.

Pyroclastic flows melted glaciers on the mountain and the melted water mixed with ash, mud and rock, causing lahars, which raced down the mountain at 60 kilometres per hour.

The lahars flowed into surrounding rivers and engulfed the nearby town of Armero – killing more than 20,000 people before they had time to evacuate.

Supervolcanoes

Nevado del Ruiz and Krakatoa were massive eruptions, but there's an even bigger volcano stirring beneath Yellowstone National Park in Wyoming in the USA.

The last eruption 640,000 years ago was 1,000 times bigger than the Mount St Helens eruption of 1980. The ground collapsed, creating a large crater called a caldera.

> **FACT**
>
> The gigantic hot spot volcano beneath Yellowstone National Park has erupted three times in the last 2 million years.

The Yellowstone caldera is 55 km by 80 km.

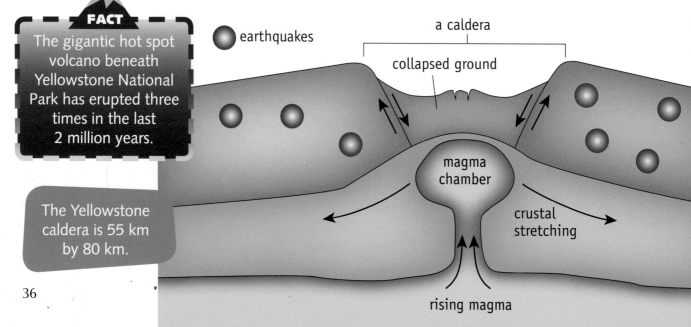

earthquakes

a caldera

collapsed ground

magma chamber

crustal stretching

rising magma

Although there's been no large eruption since then, there is volcanic activity in the area every day.

Supervolcano eruptions are very rare but if one did erupt, it could produce enough ash to block out the sun's light for several years, lowering temperatures all around Earth. Some scientists believe this happened 65 million years ago when supervolcanoes erupted in India. This is one theory for why dinosaurs became extinct.

Millions of tourists visit Yellowstone to see the hot springs and **geysers** like Old Faithful.

Volcanoes in space

The planet with the most volcanoes in our Solar System is Venus.

Venus has no oceans or plants to store gases as Earth does, so they build up, trapping more heat and making Venus the hottest planet in our Solar System. We call this a runaway greenhouse effect.

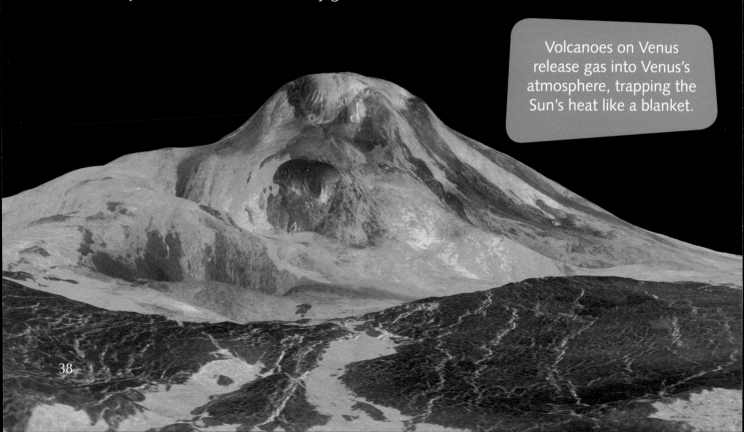

Volcanoes on Venus release gas into Venus's atmosphere, trapping the Sun's heat like a blanket.

The biggest known volcano in our Solar System is Olympus Mons on Mars.

The most volcanically active thing in our Solar System is Io, one of the moons of Jupiter. Spacecraft and telescopes have photographed erupting volcanoes, lava flood plains and calderas on Io.

Io's surface is continually being renewed by fresh eruptions of lava.

Olympus Mons – this extinct, shield volcano is more than 624 kilometres across and 25 kilometres high.

Living with volcanoes

One tenth of the Earth's population live in areas at risk from volcanic eruptions. It may sound dangerous, but there are lots of advantages to living near volcanoes.

In Indonesia, farmers grow rice around volcanoes. In Italy, vineyards are planted on the slopes of Mount Vesuvius. In Central America, coffee plantations flourish in volcanic soil.

Lava flows contain valuable resources like copper, lead, tin, gold, silver, sulphur and gemstones.

Volcanic soil contains eroded lava and ash full of nutrients, which help plants thrive.

Weather and climate

Large amounts of volcanic ash in the atmosphere can lead to unusually cold winters and summers.

It can also create spectacular sunsets as the sunlight reflects off the tiny ash particles in the air.

Enjoying volcanoes

Volcanoes are popular with tourists who bring in money to the local economy. Like Montserrat, Santorini in Greece is a popular holiday destination because of its volcano.

Hot springs warmed from heat deep within Earth are popular with tourists in places like Japan, Iceland and New Zealand.

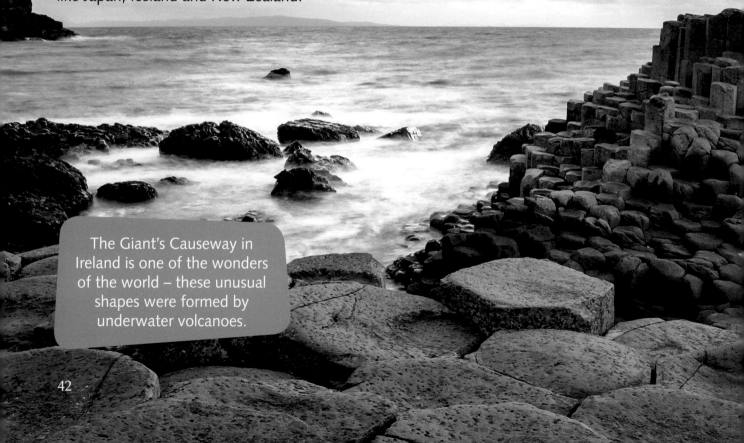

The Giant's Causeway in Ireland is one of the wonders of the world – these unusual shapes were formed by underwater volcanoes.

Geothermal power

Hot volcanic water can be pumped around homes for central heating. More than 80% of Icelandic buildings are heated this way. Hot water is also used to generate electricity.

Geothermal energy is renewable – it will never run out. Geothermal power is produced without any harmful waste products.

In a geothermal power station, warmth from the ground heats the water until it becomes steam. The steam turns a **turbine**, creating electricity.

Volcanoes can create and destroy land; they can be dangerous and even deadly. But many communities have proved that we can live with them and benefit from their valuable resources and natural beauty.

Glossary

archaeologists   scientists who dig up and study objects, bones and rocks

ash   the grey powder that's left over when something burns

atmosphere   gases in the space around the Earth

dormant   asleep or at rest

eroded   worn away

excavate   dig up and remove materials

geysers   springs that shoot hot water, steam or mud into the air

scalpels   knives with a thin, sharp blade, used by surgeons in operations

turbine   engine driven by water, steam or air

vent   opening

Index

Where in the world?

Noth America

Mount St Helens

Yellowstone

Hawaii

Montserrat

Nevado del Ruiz

Krakatoa

Pacific Ocean

Australia

South America

Iceland

Europe

Vesuvius

Asia

Atlantic Ocean

Africa

Indian Ocean

Ideas for reading

Written by Clare Dowdall, PhD
Lecturer and Primary Literacy Consultant

Reading objectives:

- discuss a wide range of non-fiction texts
- discuss their understanding and explain the meaning of words in context
- identify how language, structure and presentation contribute to meaning
- retrieve and record information from non-fiction

Spoken language objectives:

- give well-structured descriptions, explanations and narratives for different purposes

Curriculum links: Geography – understand key aspects of volcanoes

Resources: whiteboards and pens, papier-mâché and modeling materials, ICT for research

Build a context for reading

- Look at the image on the front cover. Ask children to share what they know about volcanoes and collect any technical vocabulary on a whiteboard.

- Read the blurb on the back cover together. Challenge children to attempt to answer the questions raised, focusing on *What are volcanoes?* Explain that volcanologists are scientists who study volcanoes.

- Turn to the contents page. Read it together and help children to notice how the information in this book is structured. See how case studies about real-life volcanoes are being separated using information about each different type of volcano.

Understand and apply reading strategies

- Ask children to read pp2–3 quietly, collecting new words on their whiteboards. Discuss the word "molten" and how we can work out what it means.